**One Hundred Poems
About Los Angeles**
By Troy DeVolld

Copyright © 2020 by Troy D DeVolld

All rights reserved. This book or any portion thereof may not be reproduced in any manner whatsoever without the express written permission of the publisher except for the use of brief quotations in a review.

Printed in the United States of America
First Printing, 2020

Troy DeVolld
storytroy@gmail.com

For Prudence Fenton and Patricia Harrison, with gratitude for their support and advice during the compilation and revision of the works herein.

Introduction

For the last several years, I've been in the habit of writing down observations on the experience of living in Los Angeles. Never for anyone to read, really. Just for my own reference.

Earlier in 2020, holed up at home as COVID19 shut down my industry for a stretch, I started looking at my old notebooks and hammering out little freeform observational poems, challenging myself to get a hundred of them together for a book. This book.

I hope you enjoy them.

Troy DeVolld
Valencia, California
September 17, 2020

The Notes

If line one
Could rhyme with line three
And line four
Could rhyme with line two
It would be helpful

The second stanza
Should also have the same
Number of lines as the first

We focus grouped it
And we're not real sure
People will understand
If it just reads
Like you're falling down
A flight of stairs

So if you could
Maybe
Just hit these few things
We'd appreciate it

WeHo Jesus

Here he comes
Up the drive of the Comedy Store
West Hollywood Jesus
In his white robe and sandals

I've seen him before
Posing with tourists
Hugging teary-eyed admirers
Of what he represents

And as he is received by all
With open arms
I truly wish I didn't know
His real name was Kevin*

*R.I.P. Kevin Short, "West Hollywood Jesus," 1960-2017

I Thought You Were Dead

There he goes
The sitcom star
Of long ago
Wandering Fryman
In hopes of finding
What past success
No longer provides him --
The admiration of strangers

I suspect that one day
If he makes the whole loop
Without being asked for a photo
His soul will uncouple
From his dadbod
And shoot into the sky
Where God will welcome him
With a melodic G-E-C.

Pacific

I glimpse you sometimes
From a deck or a window
And I remember
Oh, that's right, it's the ocean
We have one of those

Glitter

There's a senior
In my complex
Who dance-walks every morning
In a distressed baseball cap
With a sequined "LA" on it
And I always think
Of how it's such
A great metaphor
For the whole thing
She has
Going on
Y'know?

Tiny Kingdoms

I've never seen
So many people
With business cards
Calling themselves CEOs
Of one-man things
Run out of
Their bedrooms
And garages
But then
A little delusion
And a big dream
Is sort of
All it takes
To make it
Sometimes
Honestly

Goldenrod

I know
This is what I ordered
But now that I see it
I think that maybe
The poppyseed bun
Is wrong for it

Maybe we can change it
And just keep the rest
Except maybe the pickle
Which I thought I wanted
And it's not your fault
But

I need it like five minutes ago
If you could
That would be amazing
Hang on
I have a call
No tomato

Yes, this is
Of course
I'm with the sandwich guy

Ugh
You know what
Just give me a tea

Musso & Frank

I want to think
There's a difference
Between me
And this guy
Who just walked up to Jeff Goldblum and his sister
While they're trying to eat lunch next to me
And joke in private about his new haircut
But there isn't
Except
Fuck me if I'd be caught dead in here
In shorts and a tee shirt
Interrupting
A stranger's private moment
Because Jeff must know
He's remembered from *Jurassic Park*
No kidding

The Asterisk of Doom

There is an intersection
In Beverly Hills
Where six stop signs
Suggest to people
Who never let anyone else go first in their lives
That they must wait their turn

The patch of shattered glass
In the center
Seems to whisper
You're not going to make it
You're not going to make it
You're not going to make it

And yet, I make it.

Rodeo

A headless silver torso
Sans limbs or soul
Looks up the drive
At people in tour vans
Looking at themselves
On the sidewalks
Where no one
Carries any bags
But everyone
Is pretending to shop

The Angelino

I see you there
At the stop light
With your white shirt
And your ball cap
And your neck tattoo
Gazing unflinchingly forward

You know everyone else
Is passing through
And that you'll be here
Long after they give up
Or move to Valencia
You know the truth

Los Feliz

I'm not cool enough
I'm not cool enough
Look at those guys
Look at her
Oh my God
Why did I wear a suit

Jesus, it smells nice in here
People are having conversations
About improving themselves
Instead of how everyone else was wrong
And they were right
Exhale

Forest Lawn

Name
Date one
Date two
Sometimes a phrase
And that's pretty much the end
Of everything

For a lifetime of trying
And making and doing
Your eternal reward
Some starry-eyed strangers
Heard through the marble
Yelling "Hey, look over here"

Ba-beep, click
Ba-beep, click
Birds
More birds
Nothing
Hooray for... you know

Post-Quake Twitter

Did you feel that
Anyone feel that
Yo, was that an earthquake
I just felt an earthquake
Did you feel it
Anybody know if that was an earthquake
Holy crap
3.5
4.1
3.7
Reseda
Reseda
Where was it?
Wow
Did anyone else feel it
Earthquake
Here's how I lost 40 pounds
Link here

Tan Camry

O tan Camry
How tortured thou art
Thy headliner drooping
Thy memories of Iowa
Or some other place
A hundred thousand miles behind

You want her to make it
She's good at her craft
And you know
Because you've heard all the sides
As she runs them endlessly
And never uses the radio

You know the sticker
That says "late for rehearsal"
Makes her look like an idiot
But you believe
And you will
Even after she fades like your paint

Jennifer Love Hewitt Walks Into A Taco Bell

Bean burrito
Extra red sauce
No onions
Insignificant data
Overheard once
Remembered forever

I read somewhere
Iman likes Twix
And Martha eats bee pollen
And Molly had a gunmetal gray VW in the eighties
And yet
Is dad's birthday the twelfth or the thirteenth?

The Idea

Man
There are a lot of people
With ideas
Looking for people
To make them real
Without asking for money

Fire
Requires spark
But also fuel
So much self-described genius
Talked away
Yada-d into the ether

Eyes
On
Your
Own
Dreams
Please

Melrose Morpheus

Take the red pill
And you'll be in the business
Take the blue pill
And you'll think you're in the business
For twenty years
Until you realize you were never in it at all

The Observatory

A monument to science
To the curiosity of the human collective
And the endlessness of matter and void
She stands hillside
Her lens to infinity
Open to its lessons

They come by the thousands to see her
Not because of her wisdom
Or her knowledge of the endless
But because
You can get a good shot of the Hollywood sign
From the parking lot

Like, Manifestation, Man

Crossing Mulholland
And down toward Sunset
The Vespa ahead
Descended in the same
Fits and spurts
As the rest of us

"A friend with one
Once told me
That it's not about
If you'll ever
Lay one down
But when"

And then
Words still hanging
From my mouth
He lost control
And she yelled at me
As if it was my fault

Stargreyzing

The thing they never tell you
About coming to L.A.
Is that all your favorite stars
Are grey
And their boobs look wrong
And their beards look different
And they're much taller or shorter
Than you imagined
And you will feel old
Thinking about how they are old
And then
As if by magic
You will respect them more
As you recall the scripture
Of picture magazines
That told you all along
That they were
Just
Like
Us

The Ask

What can I do for you
Asked the friend
Now an agent
As we took our table

Nothing, I said
Just missing you
And wondering how you've been
Which did not compute

I felt like a stranger
As we ate our salads
Forgetting that here
You're supposed to need things

The Celebrity Painter

Whoever said
There is no bad art
Has never seen
The thing I'm seeing
Words
But not Ed Ruscha
Not Wayne White
Just obvious words
Like someone
Would paint on a wall
In their victim's blood
To misdirect the cops
On some police procedural

I want to believe
That I am being punk'd
And yet
Right there it says
Three thousand dollars
Which is about
What I paid
For my first car

Fuck you
I want to yell

For inviting me here
But instead
I buy a print

The Venus of Gate Four

I look out the window
Not knowing we're being cancelled
And see her roller skating
Past the gate
In a white jumpsuit
With feathered hair
And oversized sunnies
And think
For just a second
That it's 1983
Not knowing that
She's the angel of death
Sweeping over us
As the phone rings

Insta

A young woman
Tells an old woman
She's never heard of her
In that way
That young people do
Where it's less a statement
And more like the bite
Of a baby rattler
That doesn't know
How much venom
Is appropriate
Not yet understanding
The seriousness
Of being dismissed
At the end of a long career
By some influencer
Blind to her own luck

The Party

Everyone here
Is on their way up
Or out
But never down
Because those people
Aren't invited

At some point
Everyone you know
Will ascend to the rafters
Or vanish into the ether
And either way
You'll never see them again

Like drinks with like
Same dines with same
Specials with specials
Cutting a rug
With those of the same cloth
Goodbye and good luck

The Search for Signs of Accessible Life South of I-10

There are a few things I know to be true
The sun shines
The moon reflects
And Santa Monica
Is like driving to Pluto
If you live in Valencia

On the bright side
We only see the people we like
Every three years anyway
Because there's so much
Busying
To be busied here

Speedo

You know
Before I lived here
I never realized
How important
It would be
To look good in a Speedo

Because

If you look good in a Speedo
No one cares
If you can do the thing
And you can always
Blame it on
Someone less attractive

Like that guy

The Visitor

Moms
From the East
Come to visit
But all they really want to know
Is whether we have
A Target here
And what our underwear situation is
And if we can get *Ellen* tickets.

The Independent

Hooray
For that thing
With the guy
And the obfuscated story
Which must mean
It's very smart

I caught the first ten minutes
And then
Well, I've been watching the rest in parts
To savor it
And not because
It gives me a migraine
Trying to make sense
Of the thing
Because I'm smart
Which means I get it

What do you think
It means
When he says
That thing
To the ghost of the swan
In the teahouse
Not because I don't get it

But because I want to know
If you get it
Before I vote for it

That Guy From That Thing

I just
Never mind
It's just me
Probably
But then
Forget it
Somebody must like him
Because there he is again
Just like yesterday
On that clip show
With the people
Falling into the pool
And hitting themselves
In the nuts
With a rake

Another Party

So glad you could come
But you know
My friend over there
Don't look
Is kind of a big deal
So if you know who she is
Don't
You know
Say anything that might embarrass me
Because
Well, you know
She just gets that all the time
So please
And also those guys
They're all from my agency
So if you talk to them
Don't mention reality television
And actually
You know, if you could just
Hold down the fireplace
And the outer circle a little
Maybe talk to my cousin
And keep him out of everyone's hair
That would be great
And if I gave you a hundred

Could you get some more beer
Oh, and some peppered salami

Sunset

Even the dusk
Knows it has to doll up
To be seen
On the good side
Of the hill

Pinks and oranges
And yellows
Blasting silhouettes
Of the trees that don't belong here
Onto the people who don't belong anywhere else

The Los Angeles Umbrella

Patiently
She waits
For the cloudless skies
To summon her
To service

And
When the rain
Does choose to fall
She will be
In the trunk

Slow Day at the Trades

Fred Fartwinkle
Will be joining the cast
Of a show you've never heard of
On deep cable
Next season

You may have seen Fred
On this other thing
Seen only by God
For two episodes
But probably not

Hardware

There he is
Holding the bedroom door open
Eight and half pounds
Of fuck you

Engraved on the base
Superlative something
The end of the line
For validation

The subtext unetched
Still screams
Here you go, asshole
Now what

.fdr

You always did
Have a third of something to say
And the countless abandoned gardens of creativity
On your hard drive
Agree

We all laughed over
How you spoke so smugly about
All of the things you were going to do better than others
You denounced as
Hacks

Final Draft 7
On the refurbished Dell laptop
On AC life support that can't even hold a charge anymore
It's dying now
Good

The View from Runyon

Los Angeles is not palm trees
Or movie stars
Or people with money
Taking advantage
Of fresh blood

Step back

It's not studios
Or attractions
Or people taking pictures
From open-air vans
Of gates

Climb

See from the bench
A sprawling Seurat
With a million points of color
A study in magic
See it?

Hollywood Boulevard

It can't be explained
How a street
That smells like pee
And bacon-wrapped hot dogs
Was ever Mecca
For hopefuls
From all over the world
And yet
Like all tarnished things
All she needs
Is the right lighting
And a little glitter
To get the imagination going

Ruben

I always
Felt bad
About coming in
To see the man
Who mixed drinks
For Orson Welles
And ordering a Coke

I'd like to think
He knew
I respected the ceremony
More than the sugar water

Walking Tour

I have to think
People come here
Not wanting to learn
But to reinforce
What they think
They already know

And maybe see
Someone famous
Buying bagels
And Demoncrats
Plotting to overthrow Amurika
From their limos

I want to tell them
I haven't seen a limousine
Without a drunk bridal party in it
For ten years
But
You know

Eric

He stands there in the sushi place
In his unwashed track suit
His hair a mass
Of five percent debris
And stares at the menu
As no one breathes
Or looks at him
Except me

He walks to the counter
Ordering the number seven
Instructing the cashier
To put it on my tab because I looked at him
And she says no
But I nod
So she rings it up
As he scowls back
"I bet you feel real good, motherfucker"

"I do"
And in that moment
We both laugh
At how we've played each other
And yet

Somehow both come out ahead
He swings in for a shake and whispers
Almost conspiratorially,
"I'm Eric"

The Metro 750

There's a woman on the bus
With her adult son
Who perches like a gargoyle
While she laser-eyes a hole
Through a man with a grease-stained shoebox

She asks if he likes Rod Stewart
And he says no
So she threatens to have his name
Erased from the book of life
As penance for blasphemy

For just a moment
I wonder
If I'm all wrong
About the requirements
Of Heaven

Mel

To even write something bad
You must first believe
You are writing something good

These words have saved me
So many times
When nothing else would

Bottom Line

You could live
More lavishly
In Iowa
But what fun
Would that be

Better to be
Where the action is
Crashed on a sofa
In a room
Lit by Christmas lights

The point is
You haven't starved
You haven't quit
And you have
A living dream

Three Shirts Under My Name

The dry cleaner
Has a photo
Of Leah Remini
Signed
Above the counter
Just like the one
At the car wash
But you have no idea
Who those other people are
Although they all look very eager
Or serious
Or kind of surprised
Or very actorly
Their age-bleached images
Reminding you
That sometimes you get to be Leah Remini
And sometimes
You get to be one of the kids
From a Nick Jr Show
Thirty years ago
And sometimes
You get to be the viewer
Picking up shirts
And asking the counter guy
"Who's that?"

The Laptop People

They sit there in the coffee shop
Day after day
And there's nowhere to sit
It's really the only way
To get things done
When there's nothing at home
But bills and a roommate from Ohio
Who never shuts up and never goes out

The work's the thing
And while to the casual observer
It looks like fucking around
It's really the only way
To get things done
When there's nothing at home
But dues invoices and that goddamn dog
The roommate brought from Ohio

And so they labor
In the loudest place on Earth
With the banging and the foaming
It's really the only way
To get things done
When there's nothing at home
But the emptiness and the quiet
After the roommate goes back to Ohio

Penny

The neighbor down the hall
With all the plants outside her door
And the wind chimes
And the wreath
Isn't in show business
But she's been here
For thirty years now
Doing a thing
She could have done
In Florida
Without paying such a premium
And it makes you laugh
That's she's so happy
And home by five
And sings to herself
In a way that tells you
She's not preparing
For an audition
Or freaking out
About not being chosen
Or told she needs to lose weight
Because her thing
Isn't your thing
And she's amazing

Sheltered

It's the most beautiful place on Earth
You tell yourself
As you stay inside
And worry
And work
And worry some more

And you spent a little more
For the view you never see
Because of all the tv
And work
And worry
And working some more

And you wait to go out
Until it's okay to go out
But you never go out
Just waiting
And waiting
And waiting some more

A Fifty-Year-Old Man Walks Into Erewhon

You spot her
By the juice bar
And she's thin
And she's pretty
And you start to think
About how she's half your age
And she turns
To the guy
With abs on his abs
And the two-day beard
And says
The dumbest thing
You ever heard
In a chirpy get-laid voice

Then you suddenly recall
That you have done stuff
And made things
From nothing
So many times
For a living, even
That it's ridiculous
That you're even
Having this conversation
In your head

About your validity
As a human being
But you still buy
The diet tea

Fran Lebowitz and What Else

My friend from New York
Tells me I live in a place
Where no one knows anything
And the people are vapid
So I tell her
About the last time
I went to New York
And I got picked up and dropped
On a concrete ballast
By some drunk
Yelling about Saint Patrick
And leaving me a three-day limp
You can't have magic
And not have curses
And without either
What would we talk about?

The Date

She arrived
Fifteen minutes late
After losing track
Of time
Shopping
And when she asked
What I liked
About LA
I said
Everything but paying to park
Everywhere
To which she laughed
And said
She was sure
I could afford it
Because she had already
Looked up how much
TV writers make
To which I replied
I work in reality television
To which she replied
Nice meeting you
And left
Before the entrée
Which I ate

The next day
In my cubicle

Angelyne

There are a number of ways
To regard Angelyne
The billboard queen
Who made it before
You could make yourself a star
On YouTube
Or Instagram
Or TikTok
But I prefer
To be awed
Every time
She drives by
She is the slyest of winks
That reminds us
That the magic lies in knowing
It's all a show

Yours, Mine and the Truth

Everyone here knows someone they don't
And had a line on a thing that isn't
And is on the edge of a nothing something
And yet
They don't know the person's forgotten them
Or that the thing died in a conversation last November
But nobody called them
And the nothing something is still something, but different
And it's nobody's fault
And no one is lying
They're just following their interpretation
And plowing ahead
Until the someone remembers them
And the thing's out of turnaround
And the nothing's back from antimatter
And their dream lives
Because like Robert Evans said
There are three versions of every story
Yours mine and the truth
And sometimes they line up

Thaddeus

There he sat
In the park by the pier
Telling us
About the radio
He was making
To talk to God
A God made of meat
Who required the device
He'd carved out of wood

A spectacular thing
Made with craft and devotion
And not a one of us
Didn't believe
Just for a second
That there was a chance
He could be right
And that that beautiful thing
Would work someday

Ukulele

I sort of envy
Those Pasadena types
Who hide in their bungalows
From the last hundred years
With their ukuleles
And party lights
And old records
Hissing away
Yet somehow
Drive Priuses
And work
At JPL

The Shabbat Elevator

My friend at Cedars
Is recovering well
Her mortal shell
Intact for now
But it's hard not to think about forever
As I stop
On every floor
All the way down
To the end of the line
And back again
Interacting with nothing
Thinking about everything

Television City

One night
On the CBS lot
I walked out of my trailer
To see one of the cast
Sitting there
On a parking stop
By herself
In the dark
Overtaken by the vibe
Of the place
And almost in tears
That almost no one
Gets to do this
And how lucky we are
And I'm reminded
That it's true

Holding for Room Tone

They waited for the hot dog
And for the walk across Barham
And in their rental car for the hamburger
And to maybe get something signed
At the Beverly Garland

We laugh
And then we go
Wherever we go
And stand around for a living
Holding for room tone

The Hammer

I don't know
What to do
With this show
At the Hammer
With the fifteen-foot
Drawing of a crazy person
Pleasing himself
As he stares wild-eyed
Or the fabric installation
Or the video of the ocean
That's so clearly
A grant project
So I flee
To the safety
Of the permanent collection
And exhale
Safe
From the oppression
Of the bleeding edge
So craving attention

The Date

I pass them
On Hillhurst
Holding hands
And they're both
So
Young
And it reminds me
That I was young here once
And I didn't think
There was time for this stuff
Because
I needed to be something first

Silverlake

Everyone here
Has a dog
And a purpose
And the most wonderful glasses

The Optimist

My friend
Laughs at me
When I say "gee"
Or "swell"
Or throw pennies
Into fountains
At the Sherman Oaks Galleria
But for all the things
I have given up
To be here
The one I cannot shake
Is the happiness

The Capitol Records Building
From the 101 South
Still makes me cry
Same as it did the first night
And while my vision
For myself
Could stand to have its screws tightened
More than a little
And I say
Fuck
A lot more than I did

Before I moved here
It's all good

The Bank

It haunts me
For some reason
The image of
The old star
At the bank
With a bowl full of rolled change
And loose quarters
And paper clips and thumbtacks
Trying to make the deposit
Before her lunch date
So there'd be something
In the account

Beachwood

Even my tiny Ford
Feels too wide for the road
As I creep around trash bins
And keep an eye peeled
For whomever is coming
The other direction
Daring me
To play chicken

An old man and his dog
Amble ahead of me up the slope
In the middle of the street
Ear pods in and eyeballing birds
Respectively

I've no choice but to relax
Into the pace
Of the Canyon

Membership

They only want
A certain type
And so
It's cheaper if you're under 27
And you can't wear a suit
Because it's too formal
And they fancy themselves
A place for creatives
Although
All that goes on there is meetings
And it's crawling
With deal makers
And business managers
With visitor passes

Just meet me
At that dumpy Thai place we like
In the Valley
And wear
Whatever you want

Don't Blink

They just opened a new
Never mind, it closed
Have you been to the
No, I hadn't heard it moved
Dang

The Santa Monica Meter Maid

She waits
Ears open
Eyes darting
For the click
Two blocks away
A missed quarter
An absent card swipe
Her call to action

Hustle
The kind that would shame
The most enterprising young musician
Is her hallmark
Your failure
To check your watch
Her victory
Another commission

FOR LEASE

There's room enough
For everything
And yet
They're building a new this
And a new that

But what you have to understand
Is that this place
Believes in ghosts
Was built on them really
And just as a space
Once lived in by a success
Lends a false sense
Of karmic continuity
No one wants
A spot
That went bust
Selling ionized water
Or baseball cards

Off Magnolia

Just off the strip
Of thrift stores
And vintage shops
Lie streets filled
With tiny homes
Owned by grips
And script sups
And costumers
Who bought
In the 90s
When the getting was good
And now
With a new backsplash here
And a bathroom remodel there
They can finally sell them
For small fortunes
And get out of town
Before it implodes
This poem
Is brought to you
By Trulia
Which I should spend
Less time on

Content

This show is brought to you
By an Instagram influencer
And a former basketball player
And a diet soda company
And the management firm
Of Synergy, Mandelbaum and Laughlin
A subsidiary of Kablam Body Spray
Who are all keeping the money
Which is why
We can't offer you full rate
But we're sure you'll agree
It's a new world out there

Pismo

I know
That Pismo
Is not
Los Angeles
But if
I write about it
I can write off
This trip to
Splash Café
And the pastries
In Solvang
On the way back

The Front

See the celebrity on TV
With the seven-million-dollar house
And the bare walls
And the bad rental furniture
And the driveway
Full of leased cars
And cry for them
Because
It'll be gone
In three years
And they'll owe the label
Two million bucks

See the actor
In the tiny house
Out in Glendale
With the nice-enough lawn
And the carved wooden mobile
With the flying mermaids
And the thin layer of dust
On the coffee table
And smile for them
Because
They get it

Laurel Canyon

Halfway
From Studio City
To Sunset Boulevard
Someone
Has designed
An experiment
To see
How angry
You can get
At someone
Merging left
At the last
Possible
Second

Fortunately,
I happen to be
One of six people
In Los Angeles
Who can leave their house
Even three minutes earlier
Than they might need
To get somewhere
Five minutes late.

Falm

There in the building directory
Was a listing
That read
"Falm School"
And I figured
That it must be spelled that way
Because they couldn't legally
Call it "Film"
If they were just selling
The artificial version
Of the actual thing
Like "chik'n."

The Purge

Sally couldn't take the earthquakes
Jeffrey couldn't take the fires
Gilbert didn't like the traffic
Teri always felt alone

Michael missed the change of seasons
Bill's dad offered him the shop
Karen didn't like the men here
Who talked about themselves

Every farewell has its logic
But whenever someone leaves
Those of us remaining
Never seem to understand

Cancel Culture

You can never
Be sorry enough
For people
Who don't know you
And so it goes
You're over
While the masses
Who have the spare time
To speculate
Go on
Feeling smug
And forget

The Egyptian

There's a screening
Of an old film
That the cast is reuniting for
And everyone's going
In their cargo shorts
And tee shirts
To check out the ghosts
Who are still alive
So they can decide
They look terrible
Compared to sixty years ago
As if they'd be twenty forever

For Your Consideration

No one
Really knows
What to do
At a Q&A
Except ask
Predictable questions
About what so and so was like
And how did you get started

Even in a room full of people
Who ought to know better
And have had their own careers
It's still all about
Who's a hunk
And what it's like
To do the part of the thing we do
That gets the attention

Peet's

There's a woman in a Soul Cycle tee
Yelling at a kid in a Danzig tee
And he's just kind of taking it
And I wonder if either of them
Is the person they tell themselves they are

Metro

North Hollywood
The train is still
As the expressive trans woman
Tells the out-of-towners
She can hear them talking
And storms out to the next car

What was THAT
They ask me
To which I reply
You mean WHO
Just as she storms back
And reads them to filth

All I can think about
Is the story they'll tell
When they get home
To their wing joint
In bumfudge nowhere
Where they deserve to live

Bowl traffic

Highland North
On Friday Night
What was I thinking
Oh, wait
It's Winter
No problem

The Hesby

Once I lived
In a "lifestyle" building
Where every amenity came with a hashtag
And the doorbell played Snoop Dogg
And the hallways all smelled
Like bologna and weed
And the Vine stars
Shot their seven second "shows"
All over the property

On Saturday night
You could hear the supercars
Rev their engines in the street
As every sports figure's mistress in L.A.
Was retrieved for the night
Or deposited back home
To roll their eyes
As they'd pass me in the halls
#couldntwaittomove
#toomuchHerve
#elevatorsmellslikedeadstock90scologne

The Price of Being Interesting

See the rock god standing there
Seemingly no worse for wear
Wizened somewhat, I suppose
From all that stuff gone up his nose
Now every word we hang upon
In stories of his friends long gone
Imbued with character by fate
And the reckoning which happened late

Alison

Los Angeles
Is a place
Where you can die
Of empathetic nostalgia poisoning
For stuff that was already gone
Before you got here
Because that's all
Anyone talks about

Celestial Sid

Sid Grauman
Made stars out of people
With the Hollywood premiere
But the people
Wouldn't let them be
So they retreated to the heavens
And the people
Bitched about how they were
Out of touch

Burgerfornia

Choose you burger carefully
Because it's important
And you'll spend your life
Defending it

I'm a Father's Office guy
Who's baffled by the lure of In n' Out
Which might as well be a cult
The way people go on about t
With their "secret menu" everyone knows already

We love diversity
But seriously
Pick one and stick with it
Otherwise God won't know who to choose in the end times

Santa Clarita

Santa Clarita
Is the perfect place to die
Metaphorically
Chain restaurants and medical plazas
All clustered together
Conveniently
In a town
With all the character
Of a mall
Choose homes in style A, B or C
In a dazzling array of beige tones
Ready for your HOA-sanctioned personal touches
From Hobby Lobby

NYFA

"New York Film Academy"
Reads every third shirt
On the street in Burbank
Which makes me wonder
If they grade students on brand loyalty
And wearing zippered sweats
In the summer

Tram

It seems hard to believe
That all these people
Are so excited to be
On a factory tour
But then
You have to remember
That this is still magic to them
And not the place you drag into
For six a.m. call times
And without them
Where would this be?

The Porn Star in Lane Six

There she is
In the terrycloth onesie
Buying mouthwash and a bag of jellybeans
And you know her from someplace
But you're not sure where
And you wonder why
She's rolling that tiny suitcase
In a grocery store at 8am

Them

They don't want you to succeed,
This "them" and "they"
That the kids talk about
When the thing in the way is themselves

Yeah, the straw men are busy
Dashing the hopes
Of the less persistent to bits
Here in the land of dreams

Star Signs

His signature
Whittled down to a sigil
For ease of signing
Illegible
But only destined for eBay anyway

Disaster

It's an Irwin Allen Movie
Every single day
It's all on fire
And what isn't is shaking
And the stars are everywhere
And everyone's drowning
If only metaphorically
But we stay
Because Omaha wasn't cutting it
Or insert your hometown here

Chatty

There's a couch on the side of the 101
Half charcoal, half Living Spaces
Whose it was is unimportant
It's simply here now
Having its moment
As the embers waft away
Like little fireflies in the night

There's a box of stuff on the right ahead
With one side torn away
And a girl in a tube top
That looks like she's been in a dryer on "high" for a month
Is screaming for help
As she tries to recover
Her Beanie Babies
And journals
And expended MAC products
Everyone hopes for the best
But no one stops

There's just one flip flop
In the middle of the exit
Implying that some Floridian drifter
May be half barefoot
Behind a hotel nearby

And right now I'm thinking
About Taylor Negron's phrase
About how some items
Are indeed very "chatty"
About themselves

Me

Nice to meet you
Me me me me me
Me me me me me
Me me me me me
Me me me me me

Me me me me me
Me me everything you've ever done
Me me me me me
Me me saved my life
Me me me me me

Me me me me me
Maybe on your next thing me
Me me me me me
I wouldn't even ask for money
Me me me me me

Now you do all the work
While I smile blankly
And you create an experience
For me me me me
So I won't tweet you're an asshole

Review

I hated this thing
I never saw
Because it's more of the same
With that actress I hate
From that thing everybody panned
So I guess I do too

You know they're out of ideas
And nothing new works
And boy if I were running things
I'd make everything
Smart
And fresh
And not just about money

Would you read my thing
It's about a monkey
Who time travels
To the Battle of Gettysburg
I'm thinking Christian Bale in a suit
As the monkey
Great, right?

Prelude to an L.A. Ghosting

We should totally do that
Let's set it up
No I won't forget
Mind like a steel trap
See you then
And send me the thing
Because I'm completely in
And it needs to be done

Red Vines

It's a little-known fact
That television writers
If struck like a piñata
Will explode into a pile
Of delicious Red Vines
Okay
Maybe it's not a fact
But it very well could be
And we'll never know
Because the WGA
Is very explicit
In its language
About that kind of thing

Huell (Ode to Joy)

Oh wow
Look at that
It's ah-may-zing
Can you get a shot of that
This is delicious
That's incredible
Have you ever seen anything like it
Gee whiz
Oh my gosh
How long has this been here
I've never seen so many ladybugs
That was fun

About the Author

Troy DeVolld is a television producer, speaker and author from Los Angeles, California. He has worked on shows like *The Osbournes*, *The Surreal Life*, *Dancing With the Stars* and *Basketball Wives* and been quoted by or contributed to *Emmy®* magazine, *Written By*, *Time*, *Newsweek*, *The Washington Post, Entertainment Weekly* and elsewhere. He has appeared on NBC's *Today* and HLN's *Showbiz Tonight* and is currently working on a feature documentary titled REMEMBER, WE'RE NOT HERE.

DeVolld's previous titles include:

REALITY TV

AND ANOTHER THING: A BEGINNER'S GUIDE TO THE TV NOTES PROCESS

SHOULD I GO TO FILM SCHOOL?

Made in the USA
Columbia, SC
13 November 2020